ECHOES OF THE UNSPOKEN

Dikshitha Kedhari

INDIA • SINGAPORE • MALAYSIA

ISBN 979-8-89632-715-8

"I am with you, I see you."

To my brother, Sashwath

Foreword

It is a rare joy to witness the blossoming of a young talent into a voice that resonates with clarity, courage, and wisdom beyond her years. I have known Dikshitha since her childhood, and she has always been a bundle of energy and ideas, articulate in her thoughts and brimming with creativity. Today, she channels that vibrancy into this remarkable collection of poetry, offering readers a glimpse into the thoughts of this generation.

In these pages, she captures a myriad emotions and experiences — the turbulence of teenage angst, the quiet contemplation of identity, and the weight of societal expectations. Her words cut through the noise, addressing themes often left unspoken. What makes this collection particularly compelling is its honesty. Each poem is imbued with raw emotion, offering a refreshing authenticity that invites readers to reflect on their own lives. Her reflections on current affairs and their impact are especially poignant, giving voice to concerns that deserve greater attention. She has not just written poems; she has created a space for dialogue, understanding, and introspection.

As an author myself, I deeply admire the way she uses words to weave narratives that are both deeply personal and universally relatable. Her ability to illuminate the unspoken corners of life is a gift, and it is heartening to see her use it to such a powerful effect. This book is a testament to her courage and creativity, and I have no doubt it will resonate with readers across generations. It is my heartfelt hope that this collection marks the beginning of a long literary journey.

To Dikshitha, my warmest congratulations and best wishes as she steps boldly into the world of literature.

Best wishes,
Ravi Subramanian
Award-Winning Author
https://www.subramanianravi.com/

Preface

Since I was twelve, writing has been my weapon of choice to navigate and articulate my emotions and feelings. *Echoes of the Unspoken* is a collection of some of my work over this period. It is also a memoir of unacknowledged events and struggles around us, all of which I believe need to be put into words. This book has not only been an artistic journey for me but also a way to make sense of the complexity of human feelings. Whether that is in joy, sadness or fear, it is the true core of what it means to be human. Sometimes, it is the written word that has the loudest voice, and it is the written word that is heard the most. My intent in publishing this book is to give a voice to every person out there who doesn't have the freedom or the words to express themselves.

Teenagers often grapple with body image concerns and fragile friendships, which can cause anxiety and self-doubt that cloud their lives. These struggles form the focus of the first set of poems like "Architect" and "Third Friend". Such issues pile up, making them endure a silent turmoil and lose their cheer and sense of purpose. "Seventeen and Eighteen" reflects on these losses and their reticent cry for help.

The next set shifts to issues of fractured and toxic relationships and the subtly or not-so-subtly hidden domestic abuse. "Forever", "Night", and "Open Wound" express the silent battles women fight daily, forced to put on a brave face while confronting their inner and outer demons. In this day and age, as we navigate a society that is still largely patriarchal, many women and young girls are still grappling with their identity, trying to fit in and not create any ripples; themes I've tried to capture in "Other Girls" and "Mad". Many women have been rendered voiceless, and many live under the threat that they could become victims of abuse. It has become "normal" for women to remain constantly alert to protect themselves. This fear is pervasive, but societal responses are often limited to fleeting outrage when incidents make the news. I wrote "Hush" as a way to represent the atrocities being inflicted on women in Afghanistan, particularly reports of the Taliban's ban on women's voices being heard publicly. When the R.G Kar case in Kolkata came out, I wrote, "Boys Will Be Boys".

In the last set, I have tried to look at the intrinsic paradoxes of life from an internal conflict perspective in "Xoxo or Maybe Not", a philosophical perspective in "Paradox", and an egocentric perspective in "Dead Girl Underground". While the poems appear dark, I would encourage you to go deeper to find the nuances of life, strength and the need to embrace positive relationships (do read the epilogue!). Through these poems, I hope to lend a voice of support by saying, "I am with you, I see you." There is hope yet for all of us. The final poem in this collection, "Word Limit", is a reminder, a promise to myself to keep writing.

You might find yourself or someone you know in some of the words I've written or between the lines in what I have tried to convey. That is the beauty of the written word; when shared, it connects people who do not know each other in ways we may not fully understand. These poems are no longer just mine but belong to every person who finds an echo within them. To feel, to express, to understand, and to share requires strength, and I hope that when you read these poems, you will find and enable that strength, too.

Whether through writing or community work, my goal is to inspire others, build connections, and challenge boundaries. I believe that even small steps can lead to big changes – and I'm determined to keep taking them.

Thank you for picking up a copy of the book, dear reader. Let us unite in this movement and amplify these voices that are yearning to heal, resonate and rise. Let us be the change.

xoxo,
Dikshitha Kedhari

Verses Unveiled

An Architect

Everyone around her was a straight line.
Drawn by a perfectionist,
a perfect man.
Drawn with a brand-new ruler and pencil
on a new sheet of paper.
Drawn once and flawlessly.

But when she looked at the mirror,
she saw the drawing of a tired architect,
a drained man.
Drawn with a broken ruler and a blunt pencil,
erased and redrawn over and over again.
The drawing done on a crumpled sheet.

Yet when he looked at her,
he saw the work of an architect who had drawn a temple.
A gifted man.
Drawn with a ruler and a pencil that formed new shapes,
drawn and drawn again till perfected.
Drawn on a paper with the ghosts of wondrous ideas;
To him, she was the work of a broken man with magnificent
thoughts.

Envy

I walk down the hallways
but everyone's looking at your face;
My blood boils when I see you,
My vision goes red.

Jealousy is the tie that binds and binds and binds,
I want your life, what's yours now mine
because your life, it just seems to shine;
Your crown, it seems to glitter
and I just get more and more bitter.

I want it all, I want it now,
I'm the queen now, it is to me they will bow.
What's yours will be mine
until the end of time.

Third Friend

I'm the third friend in the trio,
The one who walks behind when there isn't space on the
sidewalk,
The one who is never heard when they talk;
I'm there in case they need someone to fill an extra seat,
But me being part of their laughter is a rare feat;
I'm the in-case-of-an-emergency friend,
The one who's never up on the latest trend;
I'm the one who takes their photo,
I am the third friend in the trio.

Seventeen and Eighteen

I am seventeen,
to others, my hands look pristine
but when I look at my hands, they are red
with the blood of the demons I had fed,
with the blood of the dead.

I am eighteen,
and to others, my hands look pristine
but when I sit in the fountain of blood
I realize it is not theirs but mine.
Pooled in from all the days I had lied that I was fine
and I realize I do not mourn anyone other
than the person I once was.

Forever

I thought we were forever,
But then there's a change in your tone, a slap to my face, and a
chill in my bones;
Now I'm making excuses, trying to change the topic
but every time someone brings you up in a conversation I panic.
My friends see the scars on my face
but it's not obvious to others
that I still think we are lovers.
So when these bruises start to grow,
they haven't a clue why
I can't seem to find the words to say,
"To hell with you."

Night

They ask me why I love the night
and I tell them it's because, well, I hate the light.
But the truth is
(and you know this, too):
It reminds me of you.
The stars of your twinkling eyes,
the way you used them as a disguise.
The moon of your glowing smile,
the way everything that came out of it was hostile.
And the darkness itself, of your cold embrace,
the way it hid the fact that you were two-faced.
So, when they ask me why I love the night,
I'll tell them I hate the light.

Open Wound

My wounds don't heal
the pain of the past, I still feel.
They still burn when I see you
but I doubt it happens for you, too.
I feel like I'm drowning
and my wounds, they sting.

I don't love you anymore
but my wounds are still sore;
I don't even like you like I used to,
That much is true
but my wounds, they won't heal,
The pain of the past, I somehow still feel.

Other Girls

I used to say, "I'm not like other girls,
I like black, and I play sports."
But one day, I realized
I'm exactly like other girls
because I like black and I play sports.

I used to say, "I'm not like other girls,
I'm funny, and I'm smart."
But one day, I realized
I'm exactly like other girls
because I'm funny and I'm smart.

When they told me to stop being like other girls
I realised I didn't want to;
I love other girls
and I want to be just like them.

'MAD.
UNRULY
UNRULY
MUCH
MAD
MAD.
TOO
MUCH.
TOO
MUCH

Mad

No one likes a mad woman,
Broken ceilings, torn plaster
Blatant stares, pointed fingers.

No one likes a mad woman,
The first one to scream,
The first to call you out.

No one likes a mad woman,
"Burn the witches," they said
because finally, someone dared to speak.

No one likes a mad woman
for she dares to run
and dares to win.

No one likes a mad woman
for she is unaccepting,
For she will avenge.

Hush

They don't like it when we talk,
Into our houses, we are locked;
They try to shut us up,
Back in time we jump,
Back to when we were oppressed,
Back to when we were suppressed.

They don't like it when we're seen,
Our very presence deemed obscene;
They try to hide and cover us,
Their eyes filled with lust;
It's our fault you do not know control
and we must fit into your mould.

Not to be heard,
Our silence preferred;
Not to be noticed,
To pretend like we don't exist.

Boys Will Be Boys

Not all men, but always a man.
Everywhere I go, their faces I scan,
Make sure my keys are held tight
between my fingers to put up a fight.

Not all men, but always a man.
Every woman has the same plan:
Make sure I wear a hoodie when I go out,
Make sure there are people around to hear in case I shout.

Not all men, but always a man,
Boys will be children but girls never can,
One stupid joke that's not funny,
Boys will be boys but girls, oh honey.

Xoxo, or Maybe Not

She says yes, he says no,
One is a friend, one is a foe;
He speaks his rationale, but she isn't listening,
She was expressing, but he wasn't looking;
Each one proud,
Their opinions getting loud.

He worked his pain away,
But she got drunk and with the music she would sway;
Both with pain and wrong decisions.
Their mistakes are making newer incisions,
She was emotion, he was logic,
Their arguments, more and more tragic.

She wipes her tears, he clears his throat,
One over-sensitive and the other's emotions remote,
Neither understood the other,
Behind their own walls they cower
but together they stayed, tethered by a thread,
One of them her heart, the other her head.

Paradox

Is life not a paradox
for we were born to die?
It is written in our fate
that at some point, our soul shall fly.

Is selflessness not a paradox
for it is us who feel better?
We give so we get,
We give so we feel like we've played our part in society.

Is love not a paradox
for we love just to feel loved?
We love so we feel capable of loving,
We love so we are able to fit in with the others.

Is life not a paradox
for we are born to die?
At some point, this ruse will end
and that is written in the stars in bold, capitals and underlined.

Dead Girl Underground

The people surround me,
Their grief-stricken faces I can see;
I want to ask them why
but to convey my thoughts, I can only try.
I lie there, unmoving,
My body feels like it's bruising.
Their teardrops fall on my face
but I'm stuck in one place.

Then they lower me into the ground,
My body in a box, forever bound,
The soil piles on top of me,
My soul is now forever free
but I have traded that for jailing my body,
Forever underground, eventually forgotten.

They speak their words, solemn and sombre,
They say they will miss me,
They say they will never forget,
All the memories we made, they will never regret
but now I am stuck six feet under,
Now, on the list of the dead, I am just another number.

Word Limit

I am overflowing with words I do not possess,
Words I cannot express,
No one wants to hear what I have to say
I fear.
Except for my pages,
They have been with me for ages,
Since I was twelve, evolving with the years,
Listening to my joy, my words of love, and my fears.

I am overflowing with words I do not own,
Yet I sit on the throne.
I rule the land of my paper,
Of new worlds, I am the maker,
The people bow down to me
and I live among the ones who are free.

I am overflowing with words that are not mine
and to the sheets, they are confined.
The world is forever my muse
and on the sheets, I write how it is all a ruse.

For I have the words of my own,
But only on the papers will they be shown
for it is my thoughts that are my catalyst and I am but an escapist.
Running forever from the words I say I cannot express,
Overflowing with words I do not possess.

Epilogue

After reading these poems, if you see yourselves within them, then know that it will get better. Feelings of inferiority, self-doubt, and fear stagnate and fester within us only because we fear talking about them and we believe we are alone. So, remember, you are not the only one who feels this way. This will only be recognized if more people start to speak up. When we talk and open up about our feelings or our issues, the darkness loses its hold.

Whether in relationships or decision-making, the battle between our heads and our hearts can sometimes hold us down in toxic situations where we know we deserve better but are too afraid to step away. We try to conform to societal expectations or are afraid of the stigma that accompanies standing up against oppression while sacrificing our happiness in the process. That's why we choose to stay in a group where we don't feel included, in a relationship that is flawed or stay put with inertia instead of bravely going forth into the world. It takes a lot to prioritize ourselves.

If you recognize someone you know in these poems, I hope you rise and provide strength and a safe space for them.

Changes do not occur simply by thinking about it, they happen by taking action, by being the catalyst for the change you want. Change occurs by taking that first step no matter the obstacles and pushing through them, determined to be the change you wish to see. Small steps can create ripples of change and ripples can create a tsunami.

Each one of us is the main character of our stories, and remember, every main character gets their happily ever after. It's time to stand up, speak out, and stop being afraid. Take that first step, create your safe, positive space and help others make it too. You are not alone, dear reader; there is a world of support out there for you.

So, make your voice heard, make your heart heard and make a difference.

xoxo,
Dikshitha Kedhari